HOME BUILDER'S PLANNING & MANAGEMENT GUIDE

A Personal Guide To Planning & Building Your Own Home

By

Edward J. Coppola

ISBN: 1-4033-8097-X (e-book)
ISBN: 1-4033-8098-8 (Paperback)
ISBN: 1-4033-8099-6 (Dust Jacket)

This book is printed on acid free paper.

1stBooks – rev. 1/15/04

CONTENTS

INTRODUCTION

As the title of this book indicates; this book is a guide to planning and building your home. As a guide, it intended to help you through the various phases of planning and managing your home building project.

Each of the topics covered is intended to make you aware of the building process, how it works and how they are interrelated. It is not the intention of this book to try and make you a home-building expert. There are many books written on each individual topic as well as many courses conducted in order to prepare to become an expert. It is impossible for one single book (or course) to fully prepare a person to become an expert in home building.

What this book will do for you is make you aware of the building process and aware of the questions you must ask of those people associated with this business. Follow the guidelines and suggestions in this book and you will potentially save many thousands of dollars while building your home.

Home ownership has been and still is the desire and goal of many people. To those of you who wish to own your own home, you will have various choices as to how to obtain this home. Many (if not most people) will purchase a house that is already built. This may be a new home just recently constructed or it may be a home purchased from a previous homeowner. An alternate to purchasing a ready-built home is building your own home. The building of your own home can fall into different categories:

1. Physically building the house yourself by providing your own labor
2. Acting as your own contractor by directly utilizing subcontractors and suppliers
3. Contracting with a builder to construct a house of your choice
4. A combination of the above where you contract with a builder but agree that you will provide some of your own labor or services.

There are some advantages to constructing the house yourself or having a house built according to your plan and specification. One advantage is that you, as the construction manager, will develop a house that you feel represents your lifestyle, your dream and your personality (not someone else's). Another advantage is that the time, labor or services that you directly contribute can in effect reduce the total cost of your house.

If you are not in the business of building or construction, then there are certain procedures for planning and building a house that you should learn. I will review these procedures with you in the following pages of this book. You should be prepared to plan out your house thoroughly; or you may find out (too late) that the house you ultimately end up with is not really the house you thought you were getting. Due to inadequate planning, you may also find that the final cost of the house has far exceeded your original budget.

Dissatisfaction with the different aspects of the finished house and cost over-runs are the two most common complaints or problems that the owner has after constructing his or her house. Hopefully, you will not encounter these problems if you follow the advice given in this book.

Along with building your own home goes the purchasing of a suitable parcel of land. Included in this book is a section on land analysis and investigation for those of you who will be purchasing a parcel of land. The suggestions in this section will hopefully help you choose a parcel of land that is without serious (hidden) development costs.

Building a new home is a wonderful experience that can be made a little more pleasant (and economical) by starting out with some professional advice. This book is intended to provide you with some helpful advice and to help you build a house that you are happy and satisfied with, as well as within your planned budgets.

GOOD LUCK

PART I

GENERAL

Edward J. Coppola

PLANNING

The Planning phase is one of the most important stages you will encounter. Treating this phase very seriously will help you stay on track towards your goal of a successful building program. There are many aspects to the planning of your house construction; I will briefly cover some of the more important of these aspects.

You should consider the following to help you get organized:

1. Budget—Establish how much you can afford to spend for the house
2. Style—Establish a house that you desire
3. Location—Establish an area where you want to live
4. Schedule—Establish a time frame for construction

Establishing a realistic budget, and adhering to this budget, is the most important element of home-building planning and management. Determining the amount of money you can afford to spend, obtaining this money, and spending or releasing the money properly will be an important factor as to the success or failure of your building project. Your ability to establish a budget and your ability to manage this budget will insure that you have sufficient funds to complete your house construction. Without sufficient funds you may encounter liens from unpaid subcontractors, lawsuits, an unfinished house or bankruptcy.

The budget will dictate or affect the style, location and scheduling aspects of the planning phase. Remember, in the planning phase you can modify the house style, look at a different location or change a schedule without incurring any financial loss. Once you have committed to a budget and subsequent loan amount, you are committed, and you may suffer financial consequences if the budget, planning or management is not carried out properly.

Many professionals in the building business may feel that establishing a schedule should be considered first, or determine your house style first, etc. All of the components of the planning are important and are very much interrelated. However, by establishing the schedule first, you may be unrealistically pressured into making premature decisions that can hurt you in the long term. For example; you may initially establish a schedule to be moved into your new house in 4 months. By fixing this schedule you may not spend enough time planning your house, seeking a good builder, or delaying a part of the construction when necessary to insure that you are getting what you are paying for.

Beware of builders that say that they will have you into your new home within a very short period of time (i.e. 2 months); and use this as their major selling point! Use caution when you hear this statement! A good experienced builder knows that it takes time to plan and construct a quality house. The good reputable builder will not sacrifice quality in place of time. A builder who uses the "fast schedule" selling approach, along with inadequate or poor planning, may eventually require changes and additional work to the initial

4

contract. These changes usually result in additional time required to complete the construction as well as additional costs to you.

Take the necessary time to properly plan out your house and building program by establishing a realistic budget, designing your house in detail, knowing where you want to live, and developing a detailed schedule. By planning properly, you will have a better chance to achieve your objective of building the best possible house for the available amount of money that you have budgeted, in accordance with your design plans and within a reasonable time period.

BUDGETS

A good way to start the planning process is by establishing an initial budget. First of all, you should determine the total amount of money that you can afford to spend for your house. I will assume that you will not be paying cash for the new house, but that you will require a mortgage. A further assumption is that you will be purchasing a building lot or a parcel of land upon which you will build your home.

Visit your mortgage banker or mortgage broker, very soon, to determine how much of a mortgage you can qualify for, and the total finances you can commit to building your home. It is recommended that you visit at least three different banks to determine what their terms and conditions are and to insure that you are getting the best terms and conditions for your particular situation.

Based on your current income and your current debt (loans or bills that you owe money on), your banker will be able to tell you how much money you must have for a deposit, how much money you are qualified to borrow and what your fees and expenses will be. A loan or mortgage for an existing house has different terms and conditions than a loan or mortgage for new construction, so it is important that you convey to your banker the fact that you are planning to purchase a building lot and then having a builder build a house for you. Inform the mortgage officer if you are planning to construct the house yourself by contracting directly with various subcontractors and suppliers. In this situation, the lender may require additional documentation from you and may have some additional terms and conditions concerning the loan.

Now that you know how much money you can spend, you can begin budgeting the cost of your house. You will want to determine a cost breakdown between what you will have to spend for a building lot (or parcel of land) and the house construction.

A good way to begin the budget process is to visit a real estate broker located in the community you are interested in. The broker will be able to give you a list of building lots available along with the asking selling price. Spend some time with the broker to establish a realistic average price that you will have to pay for a building lot.

The broker should also be able to give you an average square foot cost for constructing a new house. It is very important that you find out if this cost includes the cost of developing the building lot (excavations, sanitary sewer, drinking water, landscaping, etc.). If the price does not include these costs ask for a budget on completing this work. This budget will more than likely be a lump sum cost (i.e. $10,000, $20,000, etc.). Remember, this is only an average price and should be used only for your initial budgeting plan. At this time you have not completed your planning phase, so do not be pressured by the broker into purchasing or making a commitment for a building lot or a house.

With the information obtained from the broker you will be able to determine an initial budget for the cost of the house construction.

To determine the budget for your house construction do the following:

1. from your bankers information write down the total amount you can spend
2. from this amount deduct:
   fees, escrow taxes, points, attorney fees, closing costs, etc.
   (your mortgage banker will itemize these fees for you).
3. deduct the cost of the building lot and costs to improve the lot. The remaining cost is what you should have budgeted for the house construction.

From this amount it is recommended that you keep up to 10% of the money in reserve for unforeseen conditions or changes that may occur.

To determine the size of the house you can build take the budgeted cost less the 10% for reserve and divide this by the average square foot cost you received from the broker.

Here is an example:

Amount of money approved by banker mortgage officer:			$112,000
Fees to be paid:		$	2,000
Cost of building lot:		$	25,000
Cost of developing the building lot:		$	5,000
Average square foot cost from broker:		$	72

Money available from bank	=		$112,000
less fees	(-)	$ 2,000	
Total money available	=		$110,000
less cost of building lot	(-)	$ 25,000	
less cost of lot development	(-)	$ 5,000	
Money available for house construction			$ 80,000
Deduct 10%	(-)	$ 8,000	
Total		$ 72,000	

Size of house: $ 72,000 / $72 per sf. = 1,000 square foot house

You have arrived at a preliminary budget to build a 1000 square foot house for $ 80,000 on a building lot priced at $ 25,000. Remember, this is only a preliminary budget that is to be utilized for planning purposes only. Do not make any financial commitments based on this preliminary budget. The section of this book titled "Price Comparison" will help you to develop a final budget or estimate for the construction of your house.

Now that you have a good estimate of the size and cost of the home that you can build you can move on to designing your home.

DESIGN

You should plan on spending a considerable amount of time designing your house. Determine the type and style of house you want to build including the floor plan and layout. At this phase, you can do virtually anything you want with your house plans and it will not cost you any money. It does not cost anything to change lines, erase and change specifications, add or delete doors and windows, etc. However, once you sign a contract to build, it would cost you extra money to make any change no matter how large or small the change may be.

If you do not know, or are unsure as to what style house you want, drive the country side or city streets and take pictures and notes. Once you arrive at a style of house that meets your needs, you can then start planning the size, layout of rooms, and the other various aspects of the house. You can probably find a plan that you like from one of the many home magazines at your local bookstore. If you cannot find a standard type house from a magazine or book, or if you want a special design, you can hire a designer or architect to design and draw up plans for you.

Once you have the house designed and the plans finished, a specification should be developed. We will go through developing a specification latter in the book. This specification will spell out all the materials, labor, equipment, quality and standard of the components of the house.

It is not the intent of this chapter to present a complete planning course for you. The important point is that you plan, and plan very thoroughly and carefully before you contract to have your house built.

Remember, it is much easier, and certainly very much less costly, to make changes on paper. Once you and your builder or subcontractors have agreed on a price based on your plans and specifications, you are committed.

Careful planning will save you both time and money. If you desire to make changes in work that has already been completed by the builder, you can expect to pay a heavy penalty. You will have paid to have the original work completed, pay to have the work removed and pay a premium to have the new work completed. In effect a $1000 piece of work can end up costing you $5000 due to this change. If you do this often enough, you will far exceed your original budget.

It is recommended to ask builders for ideas and suggestions concerning the building of the house and all the components that will go into the house. However, know what you want, and be sure that your plans and specifications reflect what you want, before you sign a contract to build.

Edward J. Coppola

PART II

LAND ANALYSIS

Edward J. Coppola

INVESTIGATION

Before purchasing a building lot or parcel of land, it is recommended that you contact an experienced Professional Engineer to perform a site investigation and analysis. It is customary to have a clause included in your contract to purchase the property stating that the owner (Seller) gives you permission to enter onto the property to conduct necessary investigations, tests, surveys, etc.

Why spend the time and money to have someone do a land analysis for you? Because the one leading cause to building difficulties, such as large cost overruns, schedule delays and sometimes bankruptcy is a poor parcel of land! You may spend a hundred, a thousand or maybe five thousand dollars on changes to your house construction. But it is common to spend an additional $10,000, $20,000 or more for unforeseen land problems. So check it out first, before you buy the land! And have a land professional do the study for you. Do not rely on a real estate broker to give you the information you will require; they are usually not experienced in Land Analysis and Investigation.

For information regarding qualified Professional Engineers available for this type of assistance, contact the local town sanitarian or building official. The sanitarian or building official will inform you about professionals available in the area. You should contact the Engineer and inform him that you are buying land and will be requiring various investigations. The Engineer will inform you of the investigations he or she can perform, along with the fees you are expected to pay. When a professional is not available, or utilized, the burden is on the buyer to perform his or her own investigations. Be sure that you receive approval from the seller before entering the property to conduct any investigations. Also, it is worth checking with the owner or broker to determine if the owner will share in the cost of performing the investigations. You may find that they may have already conducted some of the investigations or are willing to share the cost with you.

Listed below are important factors, which should be included in all land investigations,

1. Local Zoning Regulations
2. Local Building Regulations
3. Inland Wetland Regulations
4. Method of Sewage Disposal (public or on-site)
5. Method of Water Supply (public or private well)
6. General Site Conditions
7. Roadway Status (public, private, none)
8. Environmental Conditions (hazardous or toxic waste)
9. Availability of Utilities (electric, telephone, cable TV.)

ZONING REGULATIONS

Most towns and cities have strict zoning regulations. Basically this means that the land within the town or city is divided into districts. For properties within the district boundary, a designated use, or uses, has been established. A designated use may be residential, business, farming, industrial, etc. If a parcel of land is located within a residential district, then building a house is usually allowable; a business use may be prohibited. It also follows that if a parcel of land is located within a business district a residential house may be prohibited.

The property must be confirmed that it exists in the proper zoning district to accommodate the use you have intended. This confirmation can be achieved by talking with the local zoning enforcement officer (ZEO). The ZEO can also give you information regarding other restrictions that apply to the zone. The regulations will dictate the minimum distance from the front, side and rear property boundary lines the building must be setback. The regulations will also indicate the maximum size building allowed, the minimum allowable area of the land parcel, the maximum building height as well as other particular requirements.

Some properties have additional restrictions or requirements that may not be in the regulations. These regulations are sometimes referred to as deed restrictions and can apply only to a particular parcel of property. The ZEO should be able to confirm if deed restrictions, or any other restrictions apply to your property. These restrictions are most common in private developments. The restrictions may include a minimum size house requirement, or a restriction to a particular style of house, or a restriction to the keeping of various type animals on the property.

It is not uncommon for a prospective buyer of land to discover that the intended use of the property is restricted or prohibited by zoning regulations or by deed restrictions. Therefore, check with the local ZEO or building official, before you purchase the property, to help insure that your planned house will be in compliance with the zoning regulations.

BUILDING REGULATIONS

The local building inspector can provide information concerning the building regulations and building codes. The building inspector should be made aware of the size, type and use of the building that you have proposed.

For example: you may inform the building inspector that you are planning to build a single family house, approximately 1000 square feet in size, single story with 3 bedrooms and with 1 1/2 bathrooms.

The building inspector will then inform you of the information and documentation that will be required before a building permit can be issued. You may have to submit documentation to the building official concerning Wetlands, Sanitation, Drinking Water, Zoning and building details before a building permit can be issued.

It is recommended that you submit all the paper work and applications required for the building permit before the land is purchased. Determine from the building official if a permit will be issued (or denied) once you pay the fee.

There will be a fee for the building permit. The amount of the fee will be determined by the cost of construction and the Town's fee schedule. The cost of the building permit can amount to thousands of dollars and should be included in the established budget.

If the building official will issue a permit you can move on to the next stage. If the permit is denied you should determine from the building official the reason for the denial. If the reason is due to improper filling out of forms, building design problems or fees, this problem can be easily corrected.

If the permit is denied because of a particular zoning or building regulation, the problem may not be easily or economically solved. The building official will inform you if this problem can be solved, and if so, the action you must take to correct the problem. Inform your Engineer or Attorney of the problem. They will be able to advise you of the feasibility to solve the problem and the related costs. They will also advise you, if necessary, not to proceed any further; look for another parcel of land.

INLAND WETLAND REGULATIONS

Most everyone is familiar with the concerns, nationwide, in preserving our country's wetlands. This is just not a political issue with environmentalists and developers struggling to reach a compromise or common ground. You can be assured that if wetlands exist on or near your parcel of land, no matter how large or small in size, you will be affected. Wetlands are conditions of the land; soil types, plant types and the presence of water are some conditions that determine if a parcel of land is within an Inland Wetland jurisdiction, or a Coastal Wetland jurisdiction. Depending on your particular geographic location, any one or combination of these elements will determine if the land is within the jurisdiction of Wetland regulations.

Inland Wetlands and Coastal Wetlands are conditions that must be recognized and identified. If Wetlands are present on the land you are planning to purchase, you may need special approvals before you can develop the land and build your house.

It should be determined if the town or city has its own Inland Wetland Regulations and Commission. If there are no local Inland Wetland Regulations or local commission then the State regulations and the State enforcement of the regulations may prevail. If the State regulations apply, the local building official should be able to inform you as to whom to contact for information and advice.

If the regulations exist, then a map will also be available showing the boundaries of the Inland Wetland districts. The maps should be available at the local Town hall for you to either review or to purchase. The maps should be investigated and the chairperson of the Wetlands Commission or the Wetlands Officer contacted to determine if development or building on the land is permissible. If there is any question as to potential wetlands on the property, it is recommended that you have a study conducted to determine if Wetlands are present. The Wetlands Officer should be able to give to you the name(s) of a professional soil scientist to conduct the study for you. You should contact the soil scientist to determine the schedule for completing the study and fee you will have to pay.

If there are Wetlands present you should then determine from the Wetlands Officer and your Engineer if you will need any special permits and approvals to develop and build on your property. This approval should be obtained before you purchase the property. Be careful and aware of the possible presence of Inland Wetlands on or near your property. The filling of and/or disturbing of a designated Wetland usually requires special approvals and permits. Also be aware that even though you may not be directly disturbing the Wetlands, there may be regulations that say you can not build within a predetermined separating distance from such wetlands.

SEWAGE DISPOSAL

The method of sewage disposal (wastewater) required should be determined for the particular area under investigation. The system to be used is either a public sanitary sewer (sewer pipes usually located under the roadway) or a private subsurface disposal system located on the property. The type of system to be used can be determined by asking the local health official and/or town engineer.

If a public sanitary sewer is available, then a fee is usually required in order for you to connect your property to the sewer. The important thing here is to find out if you can connect your property to the sewer. At various times, towns and cities have moratoriums on any additional connections to their sanitary sewers. Also, it is important to find out the cost of the sewer connection fee.

If there is no public sewer available to serve the property find out from the health official, or the town engineer, if a public sewer must be extended to the property or if a subsurface sewage disposal system will have to be constructed. If the public sewer must be extended, find out from the town engineer who is responsible for paying (you or the town). If a subsurface sewage disposal system is required, you will pay for both the design and construction.

A subsurface sewage disposal system is an underground sanitary sewer system, located on the property. It is located near the house and usually consists of a storage tank, distribution boxes, and pipe trenches or leaching pits. The local health official or town engineer will provide detailed information concerning the subsurface disposal system requirements.

Many states and municipalities have very strict rules and regulations concerning such subsurface disposal systems. There are many building lots and parcels of land that are unsuitable for such systems, thus prohibiting the obtaining of a building permit. It is highly recommended that you have a Professional Engineer experienced in subsurface disposal systems perform the site investigations and required designs. There will be a number of different fees for these services. The town may have an inspection fee as well as application fees. The Engineer will also have fees and should be able to give you a complete list of fees and expenses for the investigations and design. The responsibility for paying these fees will be yours unless your purchase agreement with the landowner states differently.

The four major detriments to these type systems are the presence of ledge, high ground water, poor soils and wetlands. Your Engineer should prepare a design and should investigate the property thoroughly by having deep test holes excavated to examine the soil characteristics and by performing percolation tests to determine the capacity of the soil to absorb the sewage. As stated in the previous section; it is recommended that you have a soil scientist determine if there are any wetlands present.

Obtain approval from the local health official to construct the sewage system before the property is purchased.

WATER SUPPLY

Domestic water supply to the property will be from either a public source (from a water main usually located under the road) or a private well located in the property. The type of water supply to be used can be determined from the local health official and/or town engineer.

As discussed in the previous section, if the property is to be served by a public water system determine all applicable fees from those people having jurisdiction over the public water supply system. Investigate as to where the main supply of water (reservoir or well) is located. Ask questions of the water company, local officials and neighbors concerning the quality (taste, odor, etc.) and quantity of available water.

If the water supply is to be from a private well, one way to acquire information concerning well water in the area is from neighbors. Many times a neighbor(s) can give information as to depth of wells in the area and also as to the quality of the water. This information may also be available from the local health department. However, it is important to know that water supplies are not consistent from property to property; the quantity and quality of water will vary from property to property. The only thing that can be determined at this time is the chances for obtaining a suitable source of water.

Your professional engineer and/or the local health director will make a determination as to where the well should be located on the property. This location will be based on a number of factors such as location of the sewer or septic system, house location, drains, wetlands, neighbors house location, etc.

Once the location is determined (and at such time in the construction schedule that the well is scheduled) a well drilling contractor will construct the well. Wells are constructed by well drilling contractors that have specialized equipment. You should contact well drilling contractors to determine the cost for well construction. The contractors may also have information concerning the quality of water from other wells they have constructed in the area.

GENERAL SITE CONDITIONS

The property should be investigated for adverse development conditions such as ledge and/or ground water conditions. If you and your engineer are conducting an investigation for a subsurface disposal system (see previous sections), this site investigation can be conducted simultaneously.

The presence of ledge and/or ground water is not only a problem with the sewage disposal system; ledge and high ground water conditions will also be major factors of concern with all of the other areas of the lot development.

The removal of ledge and the control of ground water can be very expensive items of work. If the site investigation does reveal these items, estimates should be obtained from an excavating contractor concerning all extra costs involved. Your engineer should be able to recommend an excavating contractor to work up estimates for you. Many times the contractor will not charge a fee for the estimates; however, it is best to confirm if a fee is required before the estimate is started.

If ledge must be removed in order to complete your lot development work, you should have determined for you the quantity of ledge and the type of ledge. Your excavating contractor should be able to tell you the quantity of ledge that is in the areas where you will be making improvements. What type of ledge must be removed? Is the ledge soft or fragmented enough so that conventional excavators such as a backhoe or bulldozer can remove it? Is the ledge hard where compressors, drills and blasting are required to remove it? Once the ledge is removed can it be utilized on-site or must it be trucked away? Is there sufficient and suitable on-site soils available to replace the ledge or must you buy fill materials from an off site source?

High ground water conditions could interfere with the normal excavations and backfill of the house excavations and required trenches. During construction, the problem may be how to remove the water from the excavations to allow the work to be performed properly. Will pumps be required or will an open drainage ditch remove the water. Is there an area to discharge the water onto your property without interfering with a neighbor's property, wetlands, public streets, etc.? What type and what size drains will be necessary to insure that the ground water will be permanently controlled to prevent entry and damage to your house and property?

Your site contractor can analyze the ledge problem and advise you of the extra work and costs that may be incurred. It is necessary that your site contractor include in the price of work removing any excess materials from your property and providing any off-site materials (fill, sand, gravel, stone, etc.) that may be required.

A building lot that is either shaped or sloped in such a manner that it will not accommodate a desired type house may have to be avoided. Many times, because of these conditions, considerable work such as extra excavations or the hauling in of fill is required to prepare the lot for the house. If you desire to have a walkout basement condition and the building lot is flat you should plan on providing additional excavations, drainage and retaining walls. If you desire to have the area around the outside of the house to be level and you have a sloping lot you should plan on having additional off-site fill materials trucked onto your property and graded.

If you currently own a parcel of land, or must acquire a particular parcel of land, then your house can be designed to fit the land. If you must have certain style, architecture and finish for your house then it is advisable to purchase a parcel of land after you have completed the house designs.

ROADWAY STATUS

You must determine if there is a means of access to your property.

Will your property border (or front) a public roadway, a private roadway, an abandoned roadway, or a right of way.

The means for accessing the property must be determined. Determine if the road by the property is a private road or a town accepted road by checking with the local building official or the town engineer. If it is a private road, find out the extra costs that are involved to maintain the road. Such factors as insurance, general maintenance, repairs, snow removal, etc. should be considered. The current property owner (or the Broker) should be able to provide you with this information.

If no roadway exists; determine if access is through a rights of way, either public or private, or if a roadway is to be built in the future. If the roadway is to be a public roadway and is currently under construction, or planned for the future, find out from the local authorities if a proper roadway bond is in place and on file. A roadway bond is insurance that the roadway and improvements will be constructed to the required specifications and accepted as a public roadway upon completion of construction.

To obtain a building permit the property must have access to a public roadway or must border a future roadway that has a bond in place. Investigate this situation before you purchase the property.

ENVIRONMENTAL

It is recommended that you try to obtain information on the presence of any hazardous waste or other environmental problems associated with the property. You can start with the current owner; if the owner indicates that there are no environmental problems, request a written verification acknowledging that there is no hazardous waste on the property and there are no environmental problems with the property. If there are known problems, obtain the verification as to what the problems are and what is required to solve and resolve the problems. You may need such verification to submit to a bank or mortgage company in order to receive a loan to purchase the land.

Also, you can inquire at the local Town hall and at the State Department of Environmental Protection agency. Many times, if a known problem exists, the agency will have it on record.

If you should acquire a property that contains a hazardous waste substance, you (not the previous owner) can be held liable for the proper removal and disposal of the hazardous waste materials.

Do your homework on this item. Resolving a hazardous waste or environmental problem can be very costly.

CONCLUSION

Before purchasing a parcel of land, for your protection, insist that a clause be written into the purchase agreement stating that the purchase of the land is contingent upon you obtaining a satisfactory engineering and site investigation report. Also, insist that a clause be written into the purchase agreement stating that the purchase of the land is contingent upon you obtaining all required permits necessary for the building and improvements. A full refund of contract deposit monies to you should be required when such approvals and permits and engineering reports are not satisfactory and/or not obtained.

It is common practice to have either or both of the above clauses written into a purchase contract. A time to complete the inspections and investigations may be required to be written into the contract. It will take some time to schedule, perform and document the investigations; so it is recommended that you use 4 weeks as a guide.

The investigations are for your protection to eliminate or minimize future development problems with the parcel of land that you purchase. The time and money you spend before you buy can be well worth the savings you may realize in the future.

PART III

BUILDING PROJECT

Edward J. Coppola

THE BUILDING PROCESS

It is very helpful to know something about the building process, before you sign a contract with a builder. However, the building process is actually a complex procedure that most people do not understand or have experience in. Project management, or the managing of the building process, is a highly technical field staffed by experts in this field. No matter what the size of a building, from a modest residential house to a complex commercial structure, the building process and management is very similar.

Planning, cost control, scheduling and quality control all play an important role in successfully completing the construction of a building. It is not necessary to become an expert in the planning and construction of a building. However, if you can understand what the major items of work or categories are, and what is the logical building process, you will have better success in working with your builder and subcontractors.

In addition, if you are planning to build the house yourself by utilizing various subcontractors and suppliers this same process will occur. However, as you can see, instead of working with just one builder you will be repeating the process with each of your subcontractors and suppliers.

The following is a list of common items you will encounter in the building process. This will prepare you to work with your builders and subcontractors.

Major Items of Work of in the building process:

Development of budgets

Development of plans and specifications

Bids (prices for construction) obtained from builders

Review and analysis of bids

Selection of a builder and subcontractors

Establishment of a schedule

Development and signing of contract with builder

Ordering of building materials

Commencement of site work

Cutting trees

Survey work

Foundation Excavation

Concrete foundation footings and walls

Foundation backfield

Commencement of building work

Delivery of framing material

Construction of floors, walls and roof

Installation of roof shingles

Installation of siding

Installation of exterior doors and windows

Commencement of electrical work

Commencement of plumbing and heating work

Installation of insulation

Installation of wallboard

Installation of floors (carpet, tile, wood)

Installation of kitchen

Paint

Appliances

Hardware

Finish electrical, plumbing and heating

Inspections

Punch list

Certificate of Occupancy (CO)

Move-in

THE SPECIFICATIONS

Specifications are a written document that describes, in detail, the components of your proposed house. The specifications will indicate the type, color, quality, manufacturer, model number, etc. of all of the equipment, appliances and materials that will be constructed into or placed into your house, foundation and building lot. The specifications will also indicate the standard and quality of workmanship to be performed by your builder and/or subcontractor(s).

The specifications, along with the house plans, will become a part of the contract you sign with the builder and subcontractor(s). The specifications will enable the builders and subcontractors to give you a more accurate bid. This will help you in making bid comparisons between builders, subcontractors and suppliers.

The following paragraphs will show you how specifications are developed and written. As an example, let us take one item that you are probably currently familiar with, and may have planned for in the construction of your house; floor carpeting. As you may know, carpeting comes in vast array of styles, types, quality, colors and costs. To indicate only that you will have floor covering of carpet does not really specify or show you what the carpeting will be like.

The specification should clarify exactly what you want for carpeting. It may indicate that Carpeting is to be:

nylon

plush

20 oz. medium traffic

3/8" thick pad

color to be......

carpeting to be installed wall to wall in the following rooms...

All labor, equipment and materials for installation to be included

How does a specification, such as the above, help you?

It spells out what you desire to have for the type of carpeting.

This informs your builder as to what you desire

It allows the builder to price the carpet accordingly.

It enables builders to give you a true bid

When the carpet is delivered to your house, you will be able

to check that it is what you had ordered

(by comparing to the specification)

A specification, such as this, should be prepared for each item of your house. As you are probably thinking; this is a lot of work! True, but what is your alternative? You must have a way to convey to your builder (in writing) what you want, the builder must have a way of accurately pricing out a cost for your house and then you must have way to determine if the builder gave you what you wanted.

SAMPLE SPECIFICATION

To help you understand the format and contents of a specification, let's develop a brief sample specification to be used as an example. This sample specification is not a complete specification for your specific use. It is intended that this example will only guide you in preparing your own particular specification as it applies to your planned house

GENERAL CONDITIONS

The builder is to pay for all costs and fees to obtain and pay for all required permits. The builder will include in the costs all costs for temporary electric and heating services. Also included are to be charges incurred during construction and until occupancy by the owner for all utility fees including electricity, heat, water, trash removal and sanitation.

The builder will include all required surveyor and engineering fees.

SITEWORK

All sitework necessary to construct the house with sanitation system, domestic water system, driveway and landscaping.

Driveway to be a maximum grade of 10%. If the grade is such that the road is higher in elevation than the house or garage the final grading is to insure that no water flows towards or into the house or garage. The driveway is to be finished with (gravel, stone, pavement, concrete) The landscaping is to consist of the following (loam & seed disturbed areas, shrubs, trees, allowance).

CONCRETE

The concrete is to be 2500 psi

Concrete slab or floor to be (3"thick, 4" thick, etc.)

All concrete ties are to removed and plugged with waterseal

FIREPLACE

Interior veneer to be (brick, field stone, etc.)

Exterior to be (brick field stone, etc.)

FRAMING

Exterior walls to be 2x6 construction

Interior walls to be 2x4 construction

Plywood sheeting on exterior walls to be 1/2"

Plywood sheeting on floors to be 3/4" T&G (glued and nailed)

All framing to be in accordance with state codes

EXTERIOR SIDING

(Specify type of siding, thickness, manufacturer, grade, etc.)
Siding to be (vinyl, aluminum, cedar clapboard, cedar shingle, etc.)

EXTERIOR TRIM

(Specify type of trim to be used)

STAIRS

(Specify type of treads and type of risers i.e. oak, pine, etc.)

INTERIOR TRIM & MILLWORK

type of trim, style of trim, paint or stain quality
type of interior doors, flush 6 panel, pine, fir, etc.

CABINETS, VANITIES & COUNTERTOPS

Indicate the type and style
Indicate the materials and the finish
There may be an allowance put aside for this item

ROOFING

Roof sheeting to be 1/2" CDX (or some other product)

Indicate type of roofing (tile, asphalt shingle, fiberglass shingle, etc.)

Indicate roof warranty

Indicate type of flashings (copper, aluminum, etc.)

INSULATION

Indicate type of insulation, what is to be insulated,

the thickness of the insulation and the "R" factor of the insulation

EXTERIOR DOORS

Type of door (wood, aluminum, etc.), style, etc.

GARAGE DOORS

Type of door (wood, aluminum, steel, etc.), size of door

WINDOWS

Type of window, manufacturer, style, etc.

Insulated glass, single or double hung, screens

Edward J. Coppola

Exterior storm sash

Color

INTERIOR WALLS

Indicate type of walls (drywall, wood panel, etc.)

Indicate thickness and finish

PAINTING

For both the interior and the exterior

Indicate what is to be painted

Indicate type of paint, number of prime and finish coats

FLOORING

Indicate type of finish flooring (hardwood, carpet, tile, ceramic, etc.)

Details on thickness, quality, etc., for each type of floor

Detail each room for each type of floor

APPLIANCES

Type of appliance to be furnished

(refrigerator, oven/range, dishwasher, etc.)

Manufacturer and style of each appliance

Color, warranty

Appliances to be hooked up and fully operational

PLUMBING

Type of supply lines and waste lines (plastic, copper, etc.)

Type of fixtures

Manufacturer, style, color, etc.

Hot water heater (type, capacity)

HEATING & COOLING SYSTEM

Type of system (electric, oil, gas, etc.)

Manufacturer, capacity, etc.

Warranty

ELECTRICAL

In accordance with all codes

Size of service (100 amp., 200 amp., etc.)

Telephone and television outlets (where and how many)

Electric fixtures (what is being supplied)

I have received many phone calls from new homeowners who are unhappy with the construction of their new house. Such complaints as; I have only one coat of paint on the walls, I thought I was getting at least two coats; the yard is a mess, I thought that the builder was going to provide a lawn landscaping; the driveway is too steep and has a gravel surface, I thought it was going to be flat and be paved; there are no gutters installed, I thought all houses had gutters; etc. etc. etc.

My first question to the caller is "what do your plans and specifications indicate?". In most cases there was no detailed plan and no specification available for the homeowner or the builder. It now becomes very difficult, if not impossible to determine if the cost of the questionable work was included in the original bid prepared by the builder. If a specification was available, the work may have been completed properly or you would have recourse to having it completed.

Remember; when you approach a builder for a price to build the house, he is very aware that you are talking with other builders and that you will probably choose the builder with the lowest bid. If you do not give the builder sufficient and detailed information for arriving at a cost, the builder will have to make assumptions. The builder will not want to include a cost for an item of work that you may not want, therefore making the bid unfavorable with another builder.

For your protection and to insure that you are obtaining and paying for what you expect and desire; be sure that the plans and specifications are complete.

SCHEDULING

A schedule should be developed for every project. A schedule defines a time frame for the designated beginning and the designated completion of the construction of the house. A schedule includes a time frame for the beginning and completion of each of the major items of work (such as the major items indicated in the specifications). The schedule can be expanded to include a time frame for the beginning and completion of various components of work included under the major items.

To those of you who are not in any particular hurry to begin building the house and moving in, a schedule may not be as important as it is to the majority of you who have to meet schedules outside of the building construction. These are rent lease termination, mortgage commitments and loan per cent changes, job relocation, etc. etc. In these instances the schedule becomes a very important aspect.

As you may recall, while we were discussing the planning stage, I mentioned that you should be cautious of the "fast schedule" selling approach. It is true that based on various conditions (which we will discuss) a builder may be able to construct the house in 3 months. Some builders may even be able to construct a house in 10 weeks. On the other hand, because of complexity and other factors, it may take 8 months to a year.

How do you develop a realistic schedule? Well, first of all you and the builder must understand and agree to what is the beginning of the schedule and what constitutes the completion of the schedule.

The builder may say that the house can be built in 3 months. You may assume that the 3 month period starts when you say "okay, go ahead" and will end when you actually move into the finished house. The builder may be actually meaning that the schedule begins when the men and equipment move onto the site and ends when the major components of the house are completed. What happens between the time you say "Okay, go ahead" and the time the men and equipment move onto the site? For one thing, in my area of the country it is not uncommon to wait 6 weeks to 3 months to obtain the various required permits before you can begin construction. When the major components of the house are completed, you cannot move in until you have obtained a certificate of occupancy (CO). Submitting the required documentation for the certificate of occupancy (CO) can sometimes take weeks. However, if the house has been constructed according to required codes, and no corrections or modifications are required, the building official can issue a CO immediately after the final inspection.

As you can see, a schedule is more than a promise or a collection of dates. It is a document that both you and the builder develop with complete understanding as to what the dates really mean.

In arriving at a time frame for the house to be built there are some preliminary (but very important) items that you should consider.

Do you have a building lot?

Are utilities available to your lot?

What is the status of the roadway?

Do you have completed plans and specifications?

Do you have a mortgage commitment?

What is required to obtain the necessary permits and how long will this take?

What time of the year is it? Will there be delays due to inclement weather?

In developing the schedule, utilization of the main headings of the specification will be helpful. At each of the specification's main category or heading, establish a beginning date and a completion date.

After you have completed your schedule, give a copy to each of your subcontractors and suppliers. Review the schedule with them and ask for their comments and recommendations and/or approval. Whenever there may be a change or revision to the schedule, be sure to contact each of your subcontractors and suppliers and furnish them with a copy of the revised schedule.

Be sure to obtain from each of your subcontractors the commitment that they will stay with the job until they have completed all of their work. If one subcontractor does not show up, or does not complete their item of work, other subcontractors may be delayed and may pull off of your project. Once a subcontractor leaves a project and starts on another project, it is very difficult to get them back. This results in a delay in schedule.

Stay in constant contact with your subcontractors and suppliers throughout the project. Always ask them how they are doing, if they are on schedule, if there are any problems and if you can be of any help. This will go a long way to helping them maintain their schedule, which will keep you on your overall schedule.

INTERVIEWING THE BUILDER

You may have a builder selected to perform the house construction for you, but would like to know a little more about the builder and his method of operation. What can you ask the builder that will give you a better insight as to how the builder will perform for you?

The following is a list of suggested questions and/or information request that you should include in your questioning or interview of the builder:

Obtain a list of most recent houses that the builder has completed. The list should include houses of similar style to the house you are planning. Also to be included with this list is the address of the house and the name and telephone number of the people the house was built for. Drive by the houses in order to get a general impression of the way the finished house looks. Telephone the owner(s) of the houses and introduce yourself. Explain that you are considering the same builder to construct a house for you and would like to ask some questions. Some questions that you would ask; are they satisfied with the house, would they use the same builder again, were there unanticipated or surprised cost over-runs, was the house construction commencement and completion on schedule? From this discussion you should get a good idea or impression of the builder's past performance.

Based on your preliminary schedule; ask the builder if your required construction schedule fits into the builder's schedule. Find out what would be the latest date a contract must be signed for the builder to complete the house according to your schedule. Let the builder know that you consider the house to be complete when all work has been completed, a certificate of occupancy obtained and ready for you to move into. If the builder can not meet your schedule find out what alternate schedule the builder can work by. Keep this alternate schedule for future reference and comparison with other builders. You may find that, for various reasons, your schedule can not be met by any of the builders you are interviewing, so a second best schedule may have to be used.

Ask the builder about the contract arrangements. Does the builder have a standard form contract? Does the builder make up a special contract or will you have your attorney make up a contract?

Ask the builder if there is a fee for reviewing the plans and specifications and for arriving at a cost for constructing the house. Find out what the fee is (if there will be a fee) and the time required for the builder to work up the cost for constructing the house.

Be sure to ask if the builder will include all sitework, utilities, fees and permits in the total cost of the house construction. Many builders will exclude these items of work or will include them as an allowance.

Ask how any extras to the work will be billed i.e.: lump sum, cost plus or time and materials.

Look for the builder who has built a house that appeals to you, who has the best references and one who will give an all inclusive price for completing all the required construction.

It is also very helpful that you and the builder appear to communicate well with each other.

Edward J. Coppola

PRICE COMPARISON

You now have your house plans, a set of specifications and a tentative schedule. You also have (or will obtain) the names of some builders you would like to contact in order to receive a price for building your house.

Many builders will work up a price based on the specifications and workmanship from a previous house that they completed; which may be different from your plans and specifications. How does this affect you? If a builder just completed constructing a house that had a much higher standard of workmanship and specification than you are requiring, the price should be higher than your budget. If a builder just completed constructing a house that had a lower standard of workmanship and specification than you are requiring, the price should be lower than your budget. It will be very helpful for you to set up a system to insure that you are making true comparisons between the builders' prices. In fairness to you (and the builders) the prices that you receive from each of the builders should be based on comparable labor, equipment, materials and workmanship.

You have already prepared for comparable prices by having the plans, specifications and building schedule (we will call the plans, specifications and building schedule the "building package") completed for each of the builders. Your instructions to the builders should be that you want a price based exactly on the plans, specifications and schedules ("base price"). Any other price the builder submits that is based on an alternate plan, specification or schedule should be in the form of an add or a deduct from the base price.

If you do not set up your system in this manner you may not be able to truly compare the prices each of the builders gives to you. In essence, you want to have each price comparison be an "apples to apples" comparison. Without this system you may be actually comparing "apples to watermelons" and not know it until it is too late for you to make adjustments.

How do you go about obtaining the price to build your house, comparing the price from the various builders and then select the builder to perform the work?

First of all, make a list of each of the builders you wish to obtain a price from (we will call this a procurement list). Included in this procurement list should be the name, address, telephone number and the contact person for each of the builders.

Without some type of record system, it can get confusing as to who was contacted, when they were contacted, and what was said or accomplished. The procurement list will help to keep a record of the date you made contact with the builder, if they will submit a price to you, the dates you had meetings with the builder, the date you submitted a building package to the builder and the date you received a price back from the builder.

This procurement list and record does not have to be very complex, but it should be detailed enough to help keep you organized. The sample list below will help you get started.

PROCUREMENT LIST

	Builder A	**Builder B**	**Builder C**	**Builder D**
address				

Tel #

contact

date contacted

will submit price (Y/N)

meeting date

building package

date submitted price

Now that you have a record of the builders that you will contact, or have already contacted, you need to set up a system for comparing the prices the builders will submit.

Try to encourage the builders to submit a base price; a price to build the house exactly as required from the building package. The builders may substitute products or material from your original specification. Do not discourage the builder from making a substitute, but be sure the cost for the substitute is shown as either an add or a deduct to the base price.

For example, you may have a 20-ounce carpet specified but the builder says they can get a much better price on an 18-ounce carpet. The base price submitted by the builder should include the 20-ounce carpet. A deduct price should also be submitted if <u>you</u> want to substitute the 18 ounce carpet. You will discover that each of the builders will have many recommendations for substituting a number of different items. Again, have the builder give you a base price and then list each of the proposed substitutes along with the cost add or deduct.

An example on how to set up a system to keep record of the prices is as follows:

PRICE COMPARISON

	Builder A	**Builder B**	**Builder C**	**Builder D**
Base price				
Add or (deduct) #1				
Add or (deduct) #2				
Add or (deduct) #3				
Add or (deduct) #3				
Total adjusted price				

Let us assume that the builders submitted the following prices and that the prices were all base bid with no changes to the plans or specifications:

Builder A - $ 107,000
Builder B - $ 110,000
Builder C - $ 108,000
Builder D - $ 108,000

Your price comparison chart would look like this:

PRICE COMPARISON

	Builder A	**Builder B**	**Builder C**	**Builder D**
Base price	$ 107,000	$ 110,000	$ 108,000	$ 108,000
Add or (deduct) #1	00	00	00	00
Add or (deduct) #2	00	00	00	00
Add or (deduct) #3	00	00	00	00
Add or (deduct) #4	00	00	00	00
Total adjusted price	$ 107,000	$ 110,000	$ 108,000	$ 108,000

This analysis is straightforward with Builder A submitting the lowest price with no changes to the building package.

Let us look at a situation where the builders want to propose some substitutions to the building package. Assume that your plans and specifications call for wood windows, vinyl siding, carpet floor covering in the living room and vinyl floor covering in the bathrooms. Builder A proposes using vinyl windows in lieu of wood windows for a savings of $1,200; Builder B proposes using cedar wood siding in

Edward J. Coppola

lieu of vinyl siding for an additional cost of $2,000; Builder C proposes using hardwood flooring in lieu of carpet for an additional cost of $700; Builder D proposes using ceramic tile in lieu of the vinyl tile for an additional cost of $500.

You should request from each builder that they give you a price for each of the 4 proposed changes. Now you can get another true comparison between the builders by adding in or deducting the changes from the base price. Your comparison chart would look like this.

PRICE COMPARISON

	Builder A	**Builder B**	**Builder C**	**Builder D**
Base price	$ 107,000	$ 110,000	$ 108,000	$ 108,000
Vinyl Windows (	1,200)	(2,000)	(2,500)	(1,800)
Cedar Siding	2,500	2,000	2,000	1,600
Hardwood Floor	600	500	700	400
Ceramic Tile	700	600	600	500
Total adjusted price	$ 109,600	$ 111,100	$ 108,800	$ 108,700

If you decide to include all the changes as a part of your building package Builder D will now be the builder with the best price.

You may decide that you are satisfied with the original specifications and you do not want to add any additional costs. However the cost savings to change to the vinyl windows looks very attractive. How will the builders' prices compare with considering only the vinyl windows change? Your comparison chart would look like this.

PRICE COMPARISON

	Builder A	**Builder B**	**Builder C**	**Builder D**
Base price	$ 107,000	$ 110,000	$ 108,000	$ 108,000
Vinyl Windows	(1,200)	(2,000)	(2,500)	(1,800)
Total adjusted price	$ 105,800	$ 108,000	$ 105,500	$ 106,200

If you decide to substitute vinyl windows as a part of your building package Builder C will now be the builder with the best price.

From this example Builder A had the best price based on the original building package. In considering the four proposed changes, you see that Builder D now has the best price and you also see a very attractive saving in using the vinyl windows. The final analysis, considering the vinyl window change, shows that Builder C has the best price.

How has this analysis helped you? Not only were you are able to compare prices between builders; you were also able to find and select a substitution that lowered your overall building price.

In this example we looked at only 4 proposed changes. It would not be uncommon to have 20 or 30 or more changes to consider. However, with this type of system it is rather easy to keep track of and analyze any number of changes.

If you are planning to be your own contractor you will set up a similar price comparison system. Acting as your own contractor you will be purchasing the materials directly from suppliers and you may contract with various subcontractors to perform the work. Your price comparison system will be more extensive; for now you must keep record of various materials as well as a number of contractors.

To help keep yourself organized, set up a complete procurement list of items that must be purchased or contracted.

As you obtain prices for each of the items, enter the price into the corresponding budget column. When you have a price for each of the items, add the budget column to arrive at a total construction budget.

A sample procurement list follows, along with an example of a finished budget.

The following sample procurement list will serve as a guide in preparing the analysis. This list is only a guide and will have to be modified according to your particular house and circumstances.

SAMPLE PROCUREMENT LIST

ITEM	BUDGET
GENERAL CONDITIONS	
permits	$
temporary electric and heating services	$
electricity, heat, water, trash removal	$
surveyor and engineering fees	$
SITEWORK	
Sitework	$
sanitation system	$
domestic water system	$
driveway	$
landscaping	$
CONCRETE	
concrete materials	$
subcontractor for concrete	
walls & floors	$
FIREPLACE	
subcontract labor & materials	$
FRAMING	
materials	$
labor	$
EXTERIOR SIDING	
subcontract	$
EXTERIOR TRIM	$

STAIRS	$
INTERIOR TRIM & MILLWORK	$
CABINETS, VANITIES & **COUNTERTOPS**	$
ROOFING	$
GUTTERS & LEADERS	$
INSULATION	$
EXTERIOR DOORS	$
GARAGE DOORS	$
WINDOWS	$
INTERIOR WALLS	$
PAINTING	$
FLOORING	$
APPLIANCES	$
PLUMBING	$
HEATING & COOLING SYSTEM	$
ELECTRICAL	$
MISC.	$
TOTAL BUDGET	$

Set up a price comparison list for each of the material suppliers and for each of the subcontractors. Instead of having Builder A, Builder B, etc. you will substitute Electrician A, Electrician B or Plumber A, Plumber B or Lumber Yard A, Lumber Yard B or whatever material supplier or subcontractor you are working with.

Shown below is an example of a price comparison for the plumbing work and the electrical work. Your analysis will be similar to the example presented earlier in this section.

PRICE COMPARISON

	Plumbing A	**Plumbing B**	**Plumbing C**
Base price	$ 4,900	$ 5,100	$ 5,200
Adjustments	---------	---------	--------
Total adjusted price	$ 4,900	$ 5,100	$ 5,200

	Electrician A	**Electrician B**	**Electrician C**
Base price	$ 4,900	$ 4,000	$ 4,400
Adjustments	---------	---------	--------
Total adjusted price	$ 4,900	$ 5,100	$ 5,200

This analysis should be completed for each of the items in your procurement list. As you arrive at a price for each of the items, insert the price into the list. After all of the prices have been inserted, add the list to arrive at the total budget for the house construction.

The following is an example as to how your finished budget may look.

ITEM	BUDGET
GENERAL CONDITIONS	
permits	$ 500
temporary electric and heating services	$ 300
electricity, heat, water, trash removal	$ 500
surveyor and engineering fees	$ 2,700
SITEWORK	
sitework	$ 5,600
sanitation system	$ 5,000
domestic water system	$ 2,000
driveway	$ 3,700
landscaping	$ 1,000
CONCRETE	
concrete materials	$ 4,000
subcontractor for concrete	
walls & floors	$ 5,000
FIREPLACE	
subcontract labor & materials	$ 3,000
FRAMING	
materials	$ 8,500
labor	$ 8,000
EXTERIOR SIDING	
subcontract	$ 1,000
EXTERIOR TRIM	$ 1,500
STAIRS	$ 1,000

INTERIOR TRIM & MILLWORK	$ 5,000
CABINETS, VANITIES & COUNTERTOPS	$ 2,000
ROOFING	$ 3,000
GUTTERS & LEADERS	$ 400
INSULATION	$ 1,500
EXTERIOR DOORS	$ 1,000
GARAGE DOORS	$ 1,000
WINDOWS	$ 4,000
INTERIOR WALLS	$ 3,800
PAINTING	$ 3,800
FLOORING	$ 3,000
APPLIANCES	$ 2,500
PLUMBING	$ 4,900
HEATING & COOLING SYSTEM	$ 5,800
ELECTRICAL	$ 4,000
MISC.	$ 1,000
TOTAL CONSTRUCTION BUDGET	$100,000

Remember, this is just your construction budget. To this budget number you must add the cost of the building lot and your reserve amount of 10%. The budget summary will look like this:

CONSTRUCTION BUDGET	$100,000
BUILDING LOT	$ 25,000
RESERVE AMOUNT	$ 8,000
TOTAL BUDGET	$133,000

If you obtain a quotation or bid for each of the items in your procurement list and by following the above procedure you arrive at a total budget that is higher than the amount you can spend, you will have to make some adjustments in either the size of the house or the type and quality of components that will be built into the house. Make any necessary adjustments and develop a new budget summary.

The important aspect of this analysis is for you to determine what the costs will be before you actually begin construction. Once you do begin construction you will be able to control and monitor the budget as outlined in the section titled "Cost Control".

THE CONTRACT

The contract is an agreement between you and your subcontractors, suppliers and/or builder stating the work and/or services that will be provided for you. The contract can be nothing more than an oral agreement in which you verbally reach an agreement or the contract can be in writing. It is strongly recommended that you have a written contract with all builders, subcontractors and suppliers with whom you are going to do business.

The plans and specifications should accurately reflect what you desire to build. The written contract that you have with your builder, subcontractors or suppliers should accurately itemize what they are providing for you, the cost of their services or products and the required schedule.

If you are acting as your own contractor, you will be entering into a number of separate contracts with various subcontractors and suppliers. The contract contents as mentioned above should be included in each of the separate contracts. If you are contracting with a single builder to do all the work you may have only one contract. Be sure to include the above information in the contract including when the builder is to begin and complete the building of your house.

The contract should incorporate into it the house plans, the specifications, and the schedule. This is accomplished by making reference to the plans and specifications in the contract. For example;

"...this contract includes all plans, specifications and schedules titled......and dated......".

The contract should make provisions for how changes will be made or how extra work is to be performed. It should also include how additional costs are determined and approved for additional work performed, or for more expensive items built into the house. The contract should also specify how you would be credited or reimbursed for approved changes in the house construction that cost less than originally contracted for. A change order form should be issued and completed for all changes.

The change order should include the following information:

1. The name and address of the contractor or supplier issuing the change order.
2. The change order number. At completion of the construction there may be numerous change orders issued. A change order number system will help you manage this system.
3. The date the change order is issued.
4. To whom is the change order issued.
5. A job or project number
6. A reference line. This may be used to give quick reference to the area of work for which the change order is issued (i.e. kitchen cabinets, appliances, etc.).
7. An area on the form to write in detail the proposed changes
8. The dollar amount of the contract. This will be the original dollar amount when the first change order is issued. For subsequent change orders, the dollar amount will include the original amount plus or minus the previous change order amounts.
9. The change order dollar amount
10. The adjusted total amount of the contact
11. The number of days the schedule will change, an increase or decrease, due to this change.
12. Signature of the contractor or supplier.
13. Your signature of approval

A following Change Order form will help you in setting up this system:

Edward J. Coppola

CHANGE ORDER

ABC CONTRACTING
address

CHANGE ORDER NO. _____   Date _____
To: _____   Job No. _____
Ref: _____
_____

You are hereby authorized to proceed with the following changes:

Amount of contract $ _____
(including extras
& credits to date)

Amount of this C.O.
increase, (decrease) $ _____

Adjusted total
new contract amount $ _____

Adjusted schedule
+\- number of days   _____

CONTRACTOR:

By: _____
signature

APPROVED:

By: _____
signature

If the change order will include a change in the schedule, be sure you check with other contractors and suppliers before you approve. An increase or decrease in time requirements may detrimentally effect another contractor or supplier. This may result in additional costs or time requirements from other contractors.

The contract should mention that all work, materials, equipment and finished systems must be in accordance with and in compliance with all required codes and regulations.

A contract can be drawn up by your attorney or you can utilize a contract drawn up by your builder. If you decide to utilize the builder's contract, it is recommended that you have your attorney review it thoroughly.

While we are on the subject of attorneys; you may be tempted not to engage the services of an attorney, either to save some money on fees or due to someone telling you that an attorney is not necessary. It is highly recommended that you engage the services of an attorney not only to draw up a building contract but also to help you with the bank documents & closing, the required documents and closing required if you purchase land and the many other problems that may arise. Remember, you are committing a significant sum of money to build your new house. You will be contracting with and working with companies and people who are very experienced in the home building industry. You will need someone who is on your side and who will represent your best interests; hire an attorney to help you.

The contract should clearly specify the guarantee or warranty to be provided by your builder. If you are subcontracting the work be sure that all of your subcontractors and vendors include a guarantee or warranty for their labor, equipment and/or materials. If the warranty is an extended manufacture's warranty then be sure to obtain all pertinent data including the telephone number and address of the department you must contact if you have a claim or problem. The warranty should indicate the covered period of time, the starting date and ending date. This period of time for individual components (such as appliances) should begin from when the product is installed and accepted by you. The period of time for the entire house, if constructed by one builder, should begin after the certificate of occupancy is issued.

Keep all the warranty information in a separate file or binder for easy reference if a problem should occur. Included in this file should be the name, address, phone number and emergency phone number of the builder and/or all subcontractors and suppliers. Also keep the names of the electrical contractor, the plumbing contractor and the heating contractors in a convenient visible area. In case of an emergency you will need this information quickly without having to search through files.

COST CONTROL

You now have all of your suppliers and subcontractors selected and contracted. You know what their prices are, you have compared the prices to your final budget, your lender has committed the funds; you are now ready to start building. The next step is to develop controls to insure that your funds do not run out before you have completed the building of your house.

A cost control system is a provision for controlling your costs by comparing and monitoring current cost against individual budget items as well as the total budget amount.

To begin the cost control system we will first separate the final budget into different categories. For convenience, the budget categories can be based on the specification categories that you have previously developed. List each of the categories and then assign a budget amount to each individual category. The total of all the category budget items will equal the total budget amount for the construction of your house.

Let us assume that your total budget for the house construction is $100,000. Take the total budget amount from the price comparison analysis you previously completed and itemize each category (the category list is from your specifications): Please note that this budget is only intended as an example and in no way is it intended to reflect what any individual item or relationship of items should be. Do not use these budget amounts for your own specific budget.

ITEM	BUDGET	COMMITTED	VARIANCE

GENERAL CONDITIONS

permits	$ 500		
temporary electric and heating services	$ 300		
electricity, heat, water, trash removal	$ 500		
surveyor and engineering fees	$ 2,700		

SITEWORK

Sitework	$ 5,600		
sanitation system	$ 5,000		
domestic water system	$ 2,000		
driveway	$ 3,700		
landscaping	$ 1,000		

CONCRETE

concrete materials	$ 4,000		
subcontractor for concrete walls & floors	$ 5,000		

FIREPLACE

subcontract labor & materials	$ 3,000		

FRAMING

materials	$ 8,500		
labor	$ 8,000		

EXTERIOR SIDING

subcontract	$ 1,000		

EXTERIOR TRIM — $ 1,500

STAIRS — $ 1,000

INTERIOR TRIM & MILLWORK — $ 5,000

CABINETS, VANITIES & COUNTERTOPS — $ 2,000

ROOFING — $ 3,000

GUTTERS & LEADERS — $ 400

INSULATION — $ 1,500

EXTERIOR DOORS	$ 1,000
GARAGE DOORS	$ 1,000
WINDOWS	$ 4,000
INTERIOR WALLS	$ 3,800
PAINTING	$ 3,800
FLOORING	$ 3,000
APPLIANCES	$ 2,500
PLUMBING	$ 4,900
HEATING & COOLING SYSTEM	$ 5,800
ELECTRICAL	$ 4,000
MISC.	$ 1,000
TOTAL BUDGET	$100,000

Edward J. Coppola

Budget and cost control systems are very important in home construction. The most common mistake that people make when spending for various components of the house is that they are always looking at or comparing to the total budget amount. What do I mean by this? In our example we are using a total budget of $100,000; this is a significant sum of money. At the beginning stages of your building you may be choosing a kitchen or bathroom system. In determining how much to spend for these items the tendency is to think that you have $100,000 to spend; so what is another $1000, $2000 or $3000 additional cost for a kitchen or bathroom. If you do this often enough you will find that you will run out of money before the house is completed. The best way to control this is by working with individual budgets for each of the house components. If you have $2500 budgeted for appliances but you really like a package that cost $3000 you will know immediately that there is a potential $500 overrun for this item and for the total cost of your house. Now you can make some choices; stay with the $2500 kitchen package, see where you have saved or can save $500 for another item(s) or come up with an additional $500 in cash (additional to the construction loan amount). If you did not have a cost control system the tendency would be to buy the $3000 kitchen package, feeling that $500 is only a small portion of the total $100,000. This is how people run out of money before they finish the house, by comparing each item against the total ($100,000) instead of against the individual item budget.

Now that you have a set up cost control system it is necessary to manage it. An efficient and easy way to manage this system is to maintain a running total or summary of monies committed. Notice that I said committed and not spent. There may be a long lead-time from the time you make a commitment to spend money to the actual time that you actually have to pay. As an example; you have met with your site contractor and agreed that the sitework will be performed for $5,600. You have committed $5,600 towards the construction of your house; however, it may be weeks or months before you actually payout or spend this money. At the time you commit the money enter the amount into the committed column of your budget analysis sheet. If there is a difference between the dollar amount of what you commit and the budget amount, enter this difference in the variance column.

The variance column will show the difference between the budget amount and the committed amount. This variance is a comparison against the budget; so enter a plus if you are over budget and enter a (-) if you are under the budget. A total of this variance column will show you, at any time, how you are comparing to the total budget. As you add and subtract the variance numbers you will arrive at either a + number which indicates the amount that you are spending above and beyond your total budget or a (-) number which indicates the amount that you are spending below your total budget amount.

As an example let us illustrate a few items; assume you have committed $5,600 for the sitework, your concrete supplier will provide the materials for $3,500 and your concrete subcontractor will charge you $6,000 to place the concrete. How will this look on your cost control system?

<u>ITEM</u>	<u>BUDGET</u>	<u>COMMITTED</u>	<u>VARIANCE</u>
GENERAL CONDITIONS			
Permits	$ 500		
temporary electric and heating services	$ 300		
electricity, heat, water, trash removal	$ 500		
surveyor and engineering fees	$ 2,700		
SITEWORK			
sitework	$ 5,600	$ 5,600	0
sanitation system	$ 5,000		
domestic water system	$ 2,000		
driveway	$ 3,700		
landscaping	$ 1,000		
CONCRETE			
concrete materials	$ 4,000	$ 3,500	(-$ 500)
subcontractor for concrete walls & floors	$ 5,000	$ 6,000	+ $ 1,000

A total of the variance column shows a + $ 500; this indicates that at this time you are over your budget by $ 500. You have some choices to make; renegotiate the amount that your concrete subcontractor is charging you, find a different subcontractor that is within your budget, or lower another item budget by $500. Be very careful about lowering another budget item without first checking and researching that you can actually complete the item for the revised cost.

As you can see, by monitoring this cost control system you will reduce the chance of running over on the total budget amount and you will reduce considerably your worry and concerns about having enough money to complete your house.

INSPECTIONS

It is recommended that you and your builder agree on an inspection program. This program would be a set schedule of times for you and the builder to review the work and schedule; to show you that the builder is providing for you what is agreed to in the contract and to help the builder better understand what you like or dislike about the completed work.

It is during these inspections and reviews that the builder can inform you of any additional costs or credits that may be necessary. Any changes, along with the costs, should be in writing and agreed to by both you and the builder before the changes are made. The building contract should also indicate that all changes are to be in writing and agreed to before such changes are made.

Keep a record of the inspections completed; including the item(s) inspected, date, approved or disapproved and changes are to be made.

The builder will also have to conduct inspections with the local building inspector or building official. These inspections are to insure that the work and materials are in compliance with the state and local building codes. The building inspector will inspect the work and either approve it or request a change if the work does not meet building code. All work must be completed and approved by the building inspector before a certificate of occupancy (CO) will be issued.

Remember, the building inspector is reviewing only for code compliance; not for quality of workmanship or materials or that the work is in accordance with the plans and specifications. It is up to you to inspect for workmanship and compliance with the plans, specifications and the contract.

If you notice, I have been saying WORKING WITH your builder. Working with your builder towards a successful project will be more beneficial to you than establishing an adversary relationship.

Many times there will be a give and take situation, for both you and your builder, during construction. If you trust your builder and he is reasonable with you, you will have a better chance to resolve the changes quickly and economically. By no means am I saying that you must be friends with the builder and give him any change and extra costs that is requested before either justification or verification is provided. What I am saying is that if you and your builder are working on a positive attitude to a successful building program, chances are that he will only present to you legitimate changes and you will be able to resolve such changes quickly and more amiably.

PROGRESS PAYMENTS

The next item to be addressed is how and when do you pay your builder or subcontractors and suppliers. Again, let us assume that you are receiving the funds through a loan or mortgage. When you received an approval for the loan you may also have received a schedule of payments as applies to the loan amount. This schedule will indicate the completed phases of work required for a release of payments. For example; completion of foundation $ 9,000, for the completion of framing $ 16,000 for the completion of site work $ 15,000, etc. These payments are called progress payments. As the work progresses through the various stages of construction, funds are released from your loan officer. Please note that the schedule of payments may not be the same as the budget or cost control system you set up.

If you are working with a single builder, the funds will more than likely be paid directly from the bank to the builder. If you are acting as your own contractor the funds may be released to you from which you will pay each of your contractors and suppliers.

At the time that you originally make application for a loan, be sure to confirm with the lender how the payment process will work. Some lenders may require that a substantial amount of work be completed before any funds are released. As an example; the initial sitework, the foundation and the rough framing including the roof and enclosure to be completed before any initial funds are released. If you are acting as your own contractor you may find that you will need interim funds to pay subcontractors and suppliers. If you are contracted with a builder, the builder may have to have access to interim funds and this may cost you additional money in interest fees. Be careful; find a lender that will work with you by dispersing funds on a regular and timely basis.

After you request a release of funds, it is a common practice for the lender to send out a representative to verify that the work has been completed and that the funds should be released. Your lender may be charging you a fee for this review or inspection; if so, be sure it is included in your budget.

Finally, have an agreement with your lender that the funds will not be released unless you request the release and that you have approved the work. What you want to avoid is the release of funds to your builder, subcontractors or suppliers if the work is not completed, or is not acceptable to you.

Before you call for an inspection and release of funds from your lender, review the completed work with you builder or subcontractors. Let them know immediately if there is a problem or if you are not satisfied. With a complete set of plans, schedule, specifications and estimate you should be able to point to the discrepancy quickly. Document and keep a record of your review including what is approved, what problems exist, and when the problems are resolved. If the work is completed and acceptable, be diligent to see that the builder or your subcontractors and suppliers are paid in a timely manner. They earned and deserve the money, this will help to insure your schedule and the continued good quality of work.

CONCLUSION

Building your own house can be a rewarding experience from both a personal achievement and from a money saving consideration. You may feel that it is a lot of work to follow the procedure outlined in this book. However, you will find that it is easier, quicker and the whole building process will be more pleasant by following the recommendations in this book. Without a plan, you will work a lot harder and have many more potential problems. Study the suggestions contained in this book, develop your plan and go to it! Don't forget to enjoy your accomplishments. Take photos as work goes along - "before and after" photos are always interesting.

Good luck and enjoy your new home for many years to come!

ABOUT THE AUTHOR

Edward J. Coppola has been associated with the design and construction industry for over thirty years. He has a degree in civil engineering and is licensed as a professional engineer in the states of Connecticut and Maine.

For the past twelve years, he has maintained a consulting engineering practice located in Killingworth, Connecticut. During this time, he has counseled many people on how to purchase land and how to plan and manage their homebuilding program.

During his career, he has designed and/or been associated with the construction of over 3,000 residential units, as well as numerous industrial and commercial projects. This experience also included responsibility for construction management, ensuring that the projects were planned, budgeted and controlled successfully.

He is considered an expert in planning, design and development of residential projects.